Look Inside a
Cave

Richard Spilsbury

Raintree

Raintree is an imprint of Capstone Global Library Limited, a company incorporated in England and Wales having its registered office at 7 Pilgrim Street, London, EC4V 6LB – Registered company number: 6695582

www.raintree.co.uk
myorders@raintreepublishers.co.uk

Text © Capstone Global Library Limited 2013
First published in hardback in 2013
Paperback edition first published in 2014
The moral rights of the proprietor have been asserted.

Edited by Rebecca Rissman, Dan Nunn, and John-Paul Wilkins
Designed by Steve Mead
Original illustrations © Capstone Global Library Ltd 2013
Illustrations by Gary Hanna
Picture research by Ruth Blair
Production by Alison Parsons
Originated by Capstone Global Library Ltd
Printed and bound in China

ISBN 978 1 406 25126 5 (hardback)
16 15 14 13 12
10 9 8 7 6 5 4 3 2 1

ISBN 978 1 406 25133 3 (paperback)
17 16 15 14
10 9 8 7 6 5 4 3 2 1

British Library Cataloguing in Publication Data
Spilsbury, Richard.
Look inside a cave.
577.5'84-dc23
A full catalogue record for this book is available from the British Library.
Acknowledgements

We would like to thank the following for permission to reproduce photographs: FLPA pp. 18 (Lars Soerink/Minden Pictures), 25 (Fabio Pupin); Naturepl pp. 5 (© PREMAPHOTOS), 6 (© Wild Wonders of Europe / Lesniewski), 7 (© Philip Dalton), 9 (© Mark Taylor), 12, 13 (© Guy Edwardes), 15 (© Stephen Dalton), 19 (© PETER SCOONES), 20 (© Jan Hamrsky), 24 (© GEORGETTE DOUWMA), 26 (© Phil Savoie), 27 (© Shattil & Rozinski), 28 (© Visuals Unlimited); Science Photo Library p. 11 (© DANTE FENOLIO); Shutterstock pp. 8 (© D. Kucharski & K. Kucharska), 14 (© Henrik Larsson), 17 (© El Choclo), 23 (© CreativeNature.nl); Superstock pp. 21 (© age footstock), 29 (© Boomer Jerritt / All Canada Photos).

Cover photograph of a big brown bat (*Eptesicus fuscus*) on the trunk of a woodland maple tree, reproduced with permission of Shutterstock (© Steven Russell Smith Photos).

We would like to thank Michael Bright and Diana Bentley for their invaluable help in the preparation of this book.

Every effort has been made to contact copyright holders of any material reproduced in this book. Any omissions will be rectified in subsequent printings if notice is given to the publisher.

Disclaimer

Contents

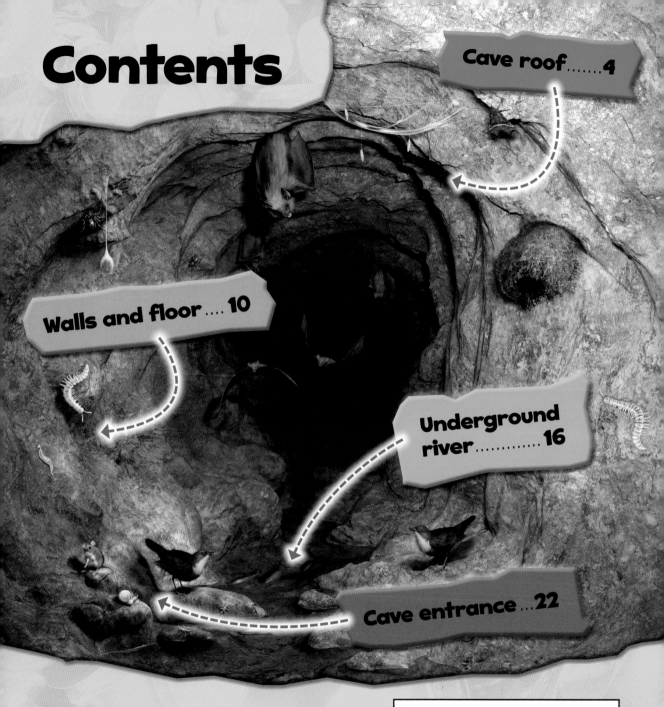

Some words are shown in bold, **like this**. You can find out what they mean by looking in the glossary.

Cave roof

Caves are dark, cool, and damp **habitats**. Habitats are places where animals and plants find food, **shelter**, and other things they need. Some animals visit or live in the roof of the cave.

Herald moths fly into caves in autumn. They shelter from the cold during the winter. In spring, they fly out of the cave to feed and have their young.

▲ Herald moths cling to the cave roof.

Bats are flying **mammals**. Some rest in caves during the day or over winter when it is cold outside. Bats hang upside down from the roof to rest!

▼ Bats grip the cave roof with their long claws.

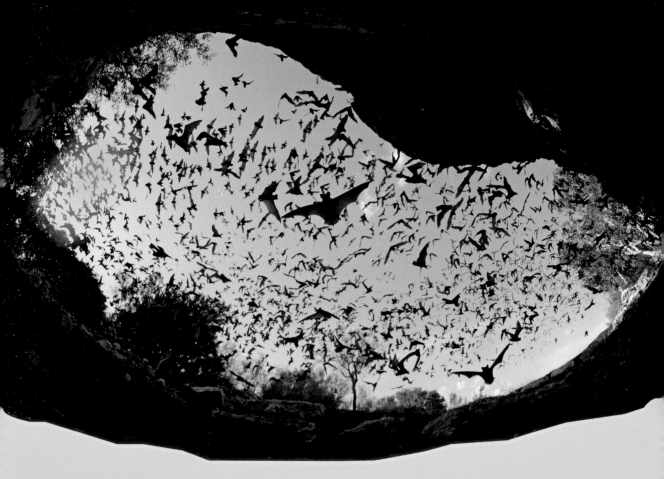

▲ Bats catch **prey** as they fly.

Bats leave the cave at night to feed. They hunt moths, beetles, and other flying **insects**. Bats squeak and listen to the **echoes** to find food in the dark.

Fungus gnats are tiny flies. In some parts of the world, **females** lay their eggs in caves. Caves are a good place to lay eggs because there is no wind or rain to blow or wash the eggs away.

▼ Adult fungus gnats live for about a week.

▲ These silky threads are a sticky trap!

After **hatching** from the eggs, **larvae** make thin, sticky threads that hang from the cave roof. Tiny **insects** get stuck on the threads. Then the larvae crawl down and gobble them up!

9

Walls and floor

Many different animals live on the dark walls and damp floor of a cave. Some are blind because there is no need to see in the dark.

Flatworms are white worms that are as flat as a leaf. They wriggle slowly along the cave floor and hunt for **larvae** and other tiny **prey**.

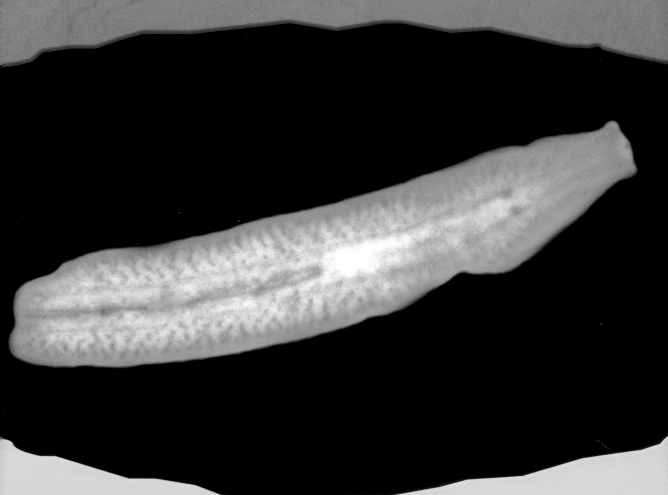

▲ Flatworms slither along on their own **mucus**.

Blind millipedes have no eyes. These long minibeasts feel their way around the cave floor using their **antennae**. They feel for tiny bits of food to eat.

▼ Blind millipedes have a soft outer shell.

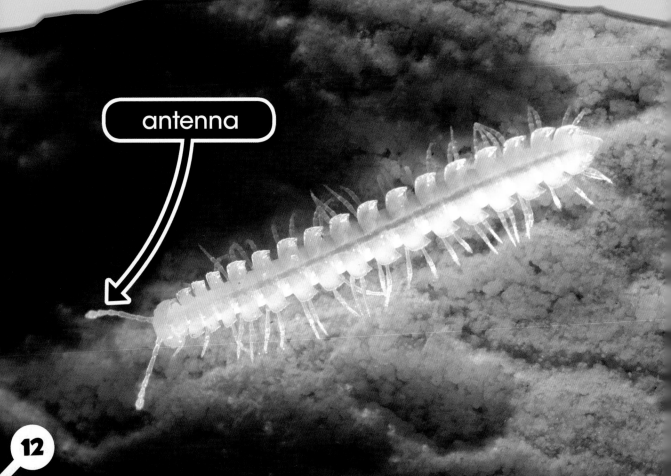

antenna

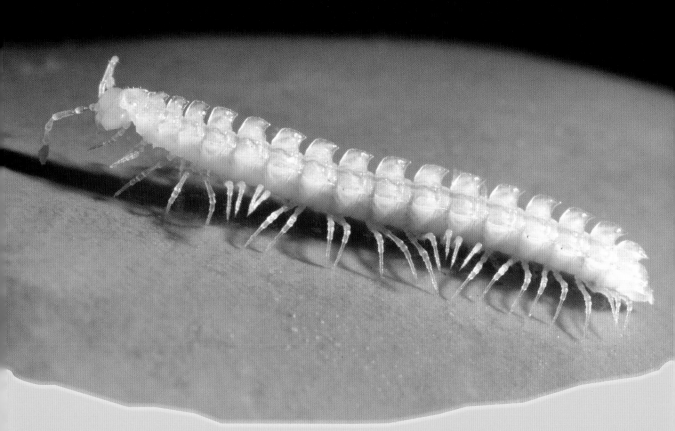

▲ Millipedes' legs move in a wave along the body.

Millipedes have four legs on each **segment**, or part, of their body. The legs along their body go forward and back in waves to move the animal forward.

Cave spiders make round webs from sticky silk threads on cave walls. The web traps millipedes and other creatures. Sometimes the spider ties up its **prey** in silk threads to eat later!

This cave ▶
spider is
spinning
a web.

▲ A female cave spider guards her egg case.

Female cave spiders lay their eggs in a silky egg case. They hang the case on a thread from the cave roof. Baby spiders break out of the case and start to make webs of their own.

Underground river

Rivers and streams flow through some caves. The cool, dark water of underground rivers is home to many different animals.

Trout that live underground are paler in colour than trout in other rivers. That is because there are no **predators** in the cave to spot them against the dark river rocks.

▲ Trout look for **insects** and shrimp to eat.

Cave shrimp have white, arched bodies and many legs. They waggle their rear legs to swim forward through the water. They bend their tails to move backwards.

▼ Cave shrimp live in flooded caves.

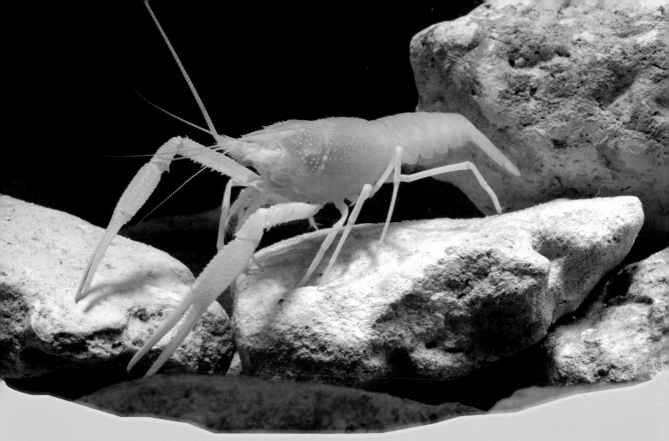

▲ Cave shrimp feel around for food in the dark.

Tiny claws on the cave shrimp's front legs help move food into its mouth. Cave shrimp eat water fleas and other **insects**. Sometimes they eat sand from the floor as it contains tiny bits of food!

Stoneflies are unusual **insects** with two tails. They live near water in caves. Stoneflies spend most of their lives as **larvae**. Then they change into adults. Adults do not survive for very long.

▼ Stonefly larvae can often be found on rocks.

▲ Stonefly larvae start life in water.

Stonefly larvae may live in cool underground rivers for years. They eat mostly water plants and use tufts behind their heads to breathe under water. Later, they crawl out of the river and change into adults.

Cave entrance

Some animals live in cave entrances. They find **shelter** there and also eat food that is washed out by underground rivers.

Mice sometimes move into cave entrances to stay out of sight of birds and other **predators**. They can also find shelter from heavy rain, wind, and bright sunlight.

▲ Some mice seek shelter in cave entrances.

The cellar snail is small with a shiny, see-through shell and a grey body. It has tiny eyes at the end of long stalks on its head.

▼ Cellar snails like damp places.

▲ A cellar snail gobbles up a dead moth.

Cellar snails slide on **mucus** trails around cave entrances in search of dead **insects** to eat. Their stomachs make special liquids that get all the goodness out of the insects' tough skin.

Dippers are brown and white birds that dive under water at cave entrances to hunt. They catch **insects** such as stonefly **larvae** washed out by underground rivers.

▼ This adult dipper has just found a meal.

▲ These dipper chicks are calling for food!

Dippers sometimes make their round nests from soft **moss** on the ledges of cave walls. The chicks that **hatch** out of the eggs are safe here. They are hidden from animals that try to eat them.

Cave habitats

Some animals, such as bats, live in lots of cave **habitats** around the world. Other animals only live deep inside a few caves. Texas blind salamanders look like white eels with legs. They live in only one American cave!

▲ Texas blind salamanders are very rare.

▲ Caves should only be explored with an expert.

Caves have interesting rocks and animals inside, but they can also be dangerous places to explore alone. It is best to visit caves in a group and be shown around by people who know the caves well.

Glossary

antennae (singular: antenna) thin parts on the heads of some animals, including beetles and lobsters, which are used to feel and touch

echo reflection of a sound off something so it can be heard again

female sex of an animal or plant that is able to produce eggs or seeds. Females are the opposite sex to males.

habitat place where particular types of living things are likely to live. For example, polar bears live in snowy habitats and camels live in desert habitats.

hatch come out of an egg

insect type of small animal that has three body parts, six legs, and usually wings. Ants and dragonflies are types of insect.

larvae young of some animals, such as insects

mammal animal that has hair and feeds its babies with milk from the mother. Humans and squirrels are types of mammal.

moss small green plant that has no flowers and grows in damp places

mucus slime

predator animal that hunts and catches other animals for food

prey animal that is caught and eaten by another animal

segment one of several similar sections making up part or the whole of a living thing

shelter place that provides protection from danger or bad weather

Find out more

Books

Bats (Usborne Beginners), Megan Cullis (Usborne, 2009)

Cave Crawlers (Landform Adventurers) Pam Rosenberg (Raintree, 2012)

Caves and Crevices (Horrible Habitats), Sharon Katz Cooper (Raintree, 2010)

Websites

See videos of animals that live in caves at:
http://www.bbc.co.uk/nature/adaptations/Troglobite

Find out more about fungus gnats at:
http://www.bbc.co.uk/nature/life/Arachnocampa

Find out about features animals have to help them survive in caves at:
http://www.caveslime.org/kids/cavejourney/caveJourneyAdaptation.html

Index